D0821783

Let's Visit the Deciduous Forest

Jennifer Boothroyd

Lerner Publications • Minneapolis

For my friends at
Lowry Nature Center

Lerner Publications Company
A division of Lerner Publishing Group, Inc.
241 First Avenue North
Minneapolis, MN 55401 USA

For reading levels and more information, look up this title at www.lernerbooks.com.

Library of Congress Cataloging-in-Publication Data

Names: Boothroyd, Jennifer, 1972– author.
Title: Let's visit the deciduous forest / Jennifer Boothroyd.
Description: Minneapolis : Lerner Publications, [2016] | Series: Lightning bolt books. Biome explorers |
    Audience: Ages 5–8. | Audience: K to grade 3. | Includes bibliographical references and index.
Identifiers: LCCN 2015039638| ISBN 9781512411898 (lb : alk. paper) | ISBN 9781512412260 (pb : alk.
    paper) | ISBN 9781512411973 (eb pdf)
Subjects: LCSH: Forest ecology—Juvenile literature. | Forest animals—Juvenile literature. | Forest
    plants—Juvenile literature.
Classification: LCC QH541.5.F6 B66 2016 | DDC 577.3—dc23
LC record available at http://lccn.loc.gov/2015039638

Manufactured in the United States of America
2-44592-21302-7/25/2017

Table of Contents

A Journey to the Deciduous Forest

Crunch, shwoosh, crunch. The leaves make noise under your feet.

How many colors do you see in this forest?

The leaves have changed colors. Red, orange, yellow, and brown leaves fall gently to the ground.

Welcome to fall in a deciduous forest. This biome changes each season.

A biome is a large area with certain kinds of plants and animals.

Deciduous forests are found mostly in North America, Asia, and Europe.

NORTH AMERICA

EUROPE

ASIA

AFRICA

SOUTH AMERICA

AUSTRALIA

■ Deciduous forest

ANTARCTICA

The trees lose their leaves in the fall.

The trees stop growing during the winter. Their bark protects them from the cold and snow.

Leaf and flower buds grow in the spring. In the summer, the trees are full of leaves again.

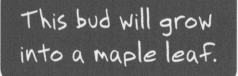

This bud will grow into a maple leaf.

Animals in the Forest

Many animals rely on trees for their food and homes. A raccoon is in its den.

Squirrels make nests in the high branches. Squirrels are very good at climbing.

Squirrels use twigs and leaves to make their nests.

This chipmunk
is eating a nut.

Chipmunks eat
nuts and seeds.
Chipmunks live
underground in holes
and tunnels. They save
food in their homes to eat
during the winter.

Many birds also live in the forest. Some birds stay in deciduous forests only during warmer weather. Some birds stay all year long.

This bright red bird is a cardinal.

Hoo, Hoo! An owl is watching from high in the tree. Owls hunt mice and shrews that scurry along the forest floor.

Woodpeckers find bugs under the bark of the trees. They use their beaks to poke holes in the bark and their long tongues to pull out the bugs.

A red-bellied woodpecker hunts for bugs.

Red foxes hunt in the forest. They live in dens and eat small animals.

Red foxes live in many habitats around the world.

White-tailed deer hide in the forest. The color of their fur blends into the colors of the forest.

Plants in the Forest

Trees are the biggest plants of the forest. Oak trees grow high in the sky. They grow acorns. These nuts are seeds that sprout new oak trees.

Squirrels and other animals eat acorns from oak trees.

Maple trees make a sweet sap. The sap flows, spreading water and nutrients throughout the tree.

These buckets catch sap that flows from the maple trees.

In the spring, wildflowers grow in the forest. Sunlight is able to reach the ground because the trees have not grown all their leaves.

There are many different mushrooms in the forest. They grow best in shaded, moist places, such as the deciduous forest. They appear on trees, on rotten logs, and on the ground.

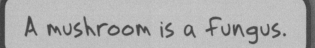

A mushroom is a fungus.

From the Ground Up

Dead leaves cover the ground in a deciduous forest ecosystem. The leaves decay. They add nutrients to the soil.

An ecosystem is all the living and nonliving things in an area.

Trees and other plants grow in the healthy soil. Bugs and small animals thrive in the soil.

Small birds and other animals
eat the insects and plants.

Animals spread
seeds all around
the forest.
The seeds grow
into new plants.

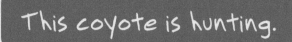

This coyote is hunting.

These small animals become food
for hawks, snakes, and coyotes.

Many plants and animals
live in the deciduous forest.
Each piece of this biome
works together!

People in the Deciduous Forest

People use trees in many different ways. In the spring, people collect sap from maple trees. They make it into maple syrup. Trees are cut into logs to make firewood. People cut some logs into lumber. Lumber is used to make buildings and many other things. Wood is also made into paper. Trees grow slowly. It is important to use trees wisely, so the forest isn't destroyed. Responsible lumber companies plant new trees to replace those they cut down. Most used paper can be recycled into new paper products.

Biome Extremes

- Smallest meat eater: least weasel (1.1 to 3.5 ounces, or 30 to 100 grams)

- Largest meat eater: Siberian tiger (660 pounds, or 300 kilograms)

- Longest life span: white oaks and other trees (about six hundred years)

- Tallest deciduous tree in North America: tulip (more than 190 feet, or 58 meters)

Glossary

biome: plants and animals in a large area, such as a desert or forest

decay: to rot or break down

deciduous: a tree that sheds its leaves each year

den: a wild animal's home

ecosystem: an area of connected living and nonliving things

nutrient: something a plant or animal needs to grow and survive

sap: fluid that moves through a plant

Further Reading

Duke, Shirley. *Seasons of the Deciduous Forest Biome.* Vero Beach, FL: Rourke, 2013.

Johansson, Philip. *The Temperate Forest: Discover This Wooded Biome.* Berkeley Heights, NJ: Enslow, 2015.

Kids Do Ecology: World Biomes—Temperate Forest
http://kids.nceas.ucsb.edu/biomes/temperateforest.html

Temperate Deciduous Forest
http://www.mbgnet.net/sets/temp

Waxman, Laura Hamilton. *Pileated Woodpeckers: Insect-Hunting Birds.* Minneapolis: Lerner Publications, 2016.

Index

Photo Acknowledgments

The images in this book are used with the permission of: © William Learman/Alamy, p. 2; © iStockphoto.com/Nataly-Nete, p. 4; © iStockphoto.com/Dieter Meyrl, p. 5; © iStockphoto.com/Vladone, p. 6; © Laura Westlund/Independent Picture Service, p. 7; © Vnlit/Dreamstime.com, p. 8; © iStockphoto.com/Pozn, p. 9; © iStockphoto.com/Krylova, p. 10; © Illg, Gordon & Cathy/Animals Animals, pp. 11, 26; © FLPA/Alamy, p. 12; © Mirceax/Dreamstime.com, p. 13; © iStockphoto.com/Steve Byland, p. 14; © iStockphoto.com/Missing35mm, p. 15; © iStockphoto.com/Chas53, p. 16; © Tom Uhlman/Alamy, p. 17; © iStockphoto.com/Frank Hildebrand, p. 18; © iStockphoto.com/notsunami, p. 19; © iStockphoto.com/Dorin_S, p. 20; © Elenathewise/Dreamstime.com, p. 21; © iStockphoto.com/naffnaff, p. 22; © iStockphoto.com/MorozVyacheslav, p. 23; © iStockphoto.com/LennartK, p. 24; © William Learman/Alamy, p. 25; © kwasny222/Deposit Photos, p. 27; © Leszczynski, Zigmund/Animals Animals, p. 30.

Front cover: © iStockphoto.com/johnnya123.

Main body text set in Johann Light 30/36.